B

C

D

AN EARLY RETIREMENT ALTERNATIVE FOR BABY BOOMERS:

"FULL-TIME RVING"

BY

TOM AND NADINE JACOBS

AN EARLY RETIREMENT ALTERNATIVE FOR BABY
BOOMERS: FULL-TIME RVING

THIS BOOK IS DEDICATED TO THE FULL-TIME RVER'S

WHO, THROUGH THEIR PIONEER SPIRIT, HAVE CHARTED

A PATH FOR ALL OF US TO FOLLOW.

OUR MOTTO:

SIX FOR COCKTAILS

FOUR FOR DINNER

SLEEPS TWO

CONTENTS

INTRODUCTION

Both of us have been in positions during our working career that did not provide much in the way of retirement benefits. Nadine worked in various levels of the medical industry and Tom has spent most of his career in the not-for-profit world. Naturally we were looking for an alternative lifestyle that would allow us to live economically and yet enjoy life at retirement. Nadine has retired from the medical industry and Tom is still working in a field that allows him to travel. Ah, the wonders of technology and what it allows us to do. Travel also allows us more time to visit family and friends across this great country and of course allows us more time to spoil our wonderful Yorkies Jake and Jill.

Our full-time adventure began two years ago. We started with a 36' 5th Wheel Trailer pulled by a Dodge 3500 Diesel Dually. We traveled about 16,000 miles in our first year going from Lincoln City, Oregon down to Key West, Florida and parts in between. Our experiences thus far have been great and we have had the pleasure of meeting and talking to hundreds of people, all with terrific stories to tell. In June of 2005 we traded to a 2004 Class A Motor Home. We did so for ease in set-up, quick access to the restroom and the ability to tow a smaller vehicle. This makes our side trips into communities we visit much more enjoyable, economical, and it certainly makes parking easier on the narrow streets of places like Key West.

Our kids had a pool going about how long we would last on the road. We have already outlasted that pool. Our plan is to remain on the road and enjoy this lifestyle as long as possible.

Our purpose for writing this book is to enhance books already published, to provide our viewpoint, and to provide a relatively short synopsis of what Full-time RVing is all about. Others have much more experience than we do but we feel that a condensed version of things you should know would be helpful to the many busy people who want to get a sense of what this is all about without initially having to spend a lot of time reading about it. Then, should you choose to pursue this exciting lifestyle, there are plenty of resources available to further assist in your planning. We have listed some of those resources at the end of the book.

1 - WHO ARE FULL-TIME RV'ERS

So what is it that happens to people who have heretofore been the pillars of society? They have been working hard, paying taxes and contributing to their communities. Many people, who because of losses in the stock market or because of real estate that has not performed to the level they had hoped for, are looking for an economical and enjoyable alternative to normal retirement. Did they wake up one morning and decide to discard all that they have worked for and begin a new type of life without some meaningful event like a lightning strike to the head? That is highly unlikely. We find that most people have done some careful planning over months and years. Although we don't have all the answers we are going to attempt to give you insight into this alternative lifestyle and some of the reasons people have made the change based on our exhaustive study of current full-timers. There are many different versions of how this lifestyle looks. It seems that the range is from total commitment of full-timing all the way to the people who maintain a stick home and travel in chunks of time (sometimes referred to as Snow-Birds). The financial arrangements are equally as varied. It seems that this new culture is having quite an impact on our society. "Baby Boomers" appear to be looking at and acting upon the Full-Time RVer lifestyle in growing numbers.

Who are Full-Time RVer's? That is a huge question and one that cannot and will not be totally answered until society sees the benefit of full-time RVer's to our culture and economy. Only then will someone be willing to fund the necessary research to get a real fix on who full-timers are and how many are on the road. When we decided to go full-time we were surprised at the number of people who were very interested in the lifestyle. We received very few negative comments. However, we do know that some people thought we might be a tad bit nuts. Some even made comments such as "so you're going to be trailer trash?" After all, the norm in society is that you must have your feet firmly planted on a piece of ground with a stick building that you can call home. That may not be as true as time goes by. In fact, many of our friends and family still living the "normal" lifestyle live vicariously through us via our bi-monthly newsletter. It is surprising how upset they get when they haven't received a newsletter in a while. Many of these folks would love to join the lifestyle and some of them are making plans to do so. The people we are talking about are from all walks of life like Doctors, Professors, CPA's, etc. We'll have a bigger list of occupations later.

We have spoken to hundreds of full-timers in our travels throughout the country. Their experiences and life before full-timing are varied and interesting. For now we want to focus on what full-timing means to the new generation,

"Baby Boomers." RVing has evolved into a culture that permits individuals and married couples to live a lifestyle that allows them to travel, enjoy life and live economically in a home that is very comfortable. A home with most of the amenities they enjoyed in their stick homes. It allows them the opportunity to retire or, in many cases, semi-retire and do the things that our parents only dreamt about.

We have also found a couple of families with one or two children, who have sold everything, bought a beautiful new 5th wheel or motor home and hit the road. These families are home schooling their children. Is a portion of our society headed towards a 21st century version of gypsies? If so it is a different breed of gypsy. These are people who have all the amenities they need, an income to support it and the ability to travel throughout the USA, Mexico and Canada, unencumbered.

We conducted an in-person and on-line survey as research for a TV documentary or series on this subject. As we talked with people and worked through the development process we determined that a natural progression would be to write a short book first and then base the TV program on it. We thank the 387 people that responded to our survey either verbally or on-line. We want to emphasize that this is not a scientific survey but it, along with our conversations with full-timers, provided us with reasonable enough data to conclude that a new culture of full-timers is emerging.

The first question we asked was how many people are living in your RV full-time? 5.1% have only one person living in the RV, 92.3% showed two people living in their RV and just 2.6% had 3 or more people living in their RV. The obvious assumption is that the vast majority of people out on the road full-time are either married or travel with a significant other. And they are doing so after the children have grown and moved on to their own lives. Our next question answered that question by telling us that of those with two or more in their RV 94.9% were married and 5.1% were just friends.

It is widely thought that full-time RVer's are people who have retired beyond the standard retirement age of 65. We were surprised to find that the average age of our respondents was 59 years old. We have to say that many of the people we have talked to on the road are in that age group. Again, this is not a scientific survey and is probably slanted towards a slightly younger group comfortable with using a computer. It does however point out that there are a tremendous number of "Baby Boomers" looking for an alternative lifestyle.

We also learned that there are many well educated people out on the road. Our survey showed that 12% had at least a high school education. 33% had some college and/or attended advance training classes for their occupation. A majority 55% of the respondents have college degrees. Of those with college degrees approximately 16% held an Associates Degree, about 53% a Bachelor Degree, 26% hold a Masters Degree and 5% are at the Doctorate level. Additional certificates earned by the respondents include:

Registered Nurse, Non-profit Management, Welding Equipment Maintenance, Commercial Pilot, US Navy Instructor, Realty, Journeyman Die Maker, Registered Pharmacist, and Certified Family Mediator.

Occupations prior to going full-time are varied. The following list may be a bit long but will give you a sense of what people did prior to hitting the road:

Grant Administrator, Psychiatric Social Worker, Secretary, Governmental Manager, Transportation Planner, Registered Nurse, Electrical Assembler, Entrepreneur, Professor, Medical Administrators, Non-profit Administrator, Television Production, GM of Sanitation Dept., Skilled Trades, Commercial Pilots, Deputy Director of Finance, Motivational Speaker/Sales Trainer, Instructor, Realtor, Attorney, Computer Programmers, Admin. Assistant, Manager, Government Senior Scientist, Property Manager, Teacher, Self Employed, State Computer Help Manager, State Computer Lab, Wireless Co. Manager, Merchandiser, Software Consultant, Homemaker, Wildlife Biologist, Army Officer, Police Officer, Company Owner, Master Electrician, Administrative Assistant, Chief of Police, Elementary school Principal, Insurance Agent, City Administrator, Senior

Automotive Engineer, Public Relations Director, Construction Superintendent, Purchasing Supervisor, Dental assistant, Mining Engineer, IT Manager, Respiratory Therapist, Aerospace Engineer, Baker, Teaching Assistant, Tech Manager in Beverage Industry, Railroad Conductor, Pharmacist, Social Worker/Mediator. As you can see many full-timers are well educated people from all walks of life.

We thought it might be interesting to find out the income levels of people prior to going full-time. We asked the question in our survey and Movinon.net asked the same question of those visiting their website. We thank them for sharing the results of their survey. Although there were some differences we both showed that over 63% of the respondents had family incomes of over $50,000 per year over 25% earned $100,000 and over. Our results are as follows for income prior to going full-time:

0 - $20,000	2.8%
$20,000 - $30,000	21%
$30,000 - $40,000	3.9%
$40,000 - $50,000	8.9%
$50,000 - $75,000	21.2%
$75,000 - $100,000	16.5%
$100,000+	25.7%

Again these figures and figures from other surveys are not scientific so can vary based on what surveys you read. We can however attest to the fact that many of the people we talked with face to face appear to be in the upper income level. Just in case some people reading this might think that we only park our RV in upscale RV parks you could not be further from the truth. We stay at very few upscale parks. We use Passport America 90% of the time. Not to say there are not many nice parks as part of that plan but they are not on the level of some of the Southern California parks around Palm Springs for example. The Passport America parks are where we met a large number of the people we talked with. For those who do not know about Passport America we will discuss it later on in the book.

So what are the sources of income for full-timers? Retired people naturally lead the list. Several also use more than one source of revenue. Many people received either early retirement or invested well enough to retire early. 35.2% are living on a company retirement pension, 29.7% use Social Security, 24.3% use savings as a source of income, 6.8% are doing some type of full-time work and 4% are doing part time work. Some people use the workamper.com program or other similar programs to supplement their income. Some also supplement their income via rentals, Workers Comp., VA Disability, eBay, Insurance Sales Renewals and the good ole 401K.

Monthly budgets are an absolute necessity when you go full-time. The last thing you need is a surprise as you approach the end of the month and the money has run out. Only 2.6% of respondents live on a monthly budget of $1,000 or less. Almost 23% are able to manage a budget of $1,000 to $2,500, 56% live within the $2,500 to $5,000 level and 2.6% scrape by on $7,500 to $10,000 per month. You will see as you read on that there are many ways to save and work within whatever budget you have.

Health Care is obviously a huge issue to be dealt with prior to making a decision. You will see as you read on that there are many ways to save and work within whatever budget you will have when going full-time. As we retire earlier and company provided insurance at retirement is becoming a thing of the past, finding quality health insurance at an affordable price can be a challenge. Fortunately a large number of our respondents still have company paid health insurance available to them. Over 43% indicated that they are still covered by the company they retired from. We were surprised to see that only 32% were on Medicare. That falls in line with the average age we discussed earlier. Those not eligible for Medicare and do not have company provided insurance numbered about 23%. These folks have private insurance plans. Only about 2% indicated that they had no insurance at all. Obviously some people use multiple insurance sources. Others are supplementing other policies with Medicare

Supplements, Tricare, Cobra and VA Insurance. We will cover health insurance later in the book. The other challenge and expense related to health coverage has to do with medications. We are blessed with medical advances which allow us to live long healthy lives by taking medications to keep numerous health problems in check. The only problem is that many of those medications are very expensive. No doubt there are many people who are stuck in their current lifestyle because of access to medications through a company insurance policy. At this point over 63% of the respondents indicated that they purchase medications through health insurance coverage. The remaining people either pay cash for their medications or they go without. We all know about the controversy of purchasing medications in Mexico and Canada. It is an alternative that many people are using if they have the opportunity to visit these countries. Full-time RVer's have that opportunity available to them. Approximately 4% of the people responding to our survey have purchased medications from Canada. Over 12% visit Mexico to buy their medications. Later on we will talk more about this and give you some pointers on what not to attempt to buy in foreign countries. We were astonished when we crossed the border into Los Algodones, Mexico, just outside of Yuma, Arizona, to see how many Americans were either buying medications or getting dental and optometry work done. Apparently this same situation is occurring in towns all across the Mexican/American border. When you see lines of people many blocks long waiting to go through customs with bags of medications you have to think that our country needs to take action, and now, to make medications more reasonably priced. It is a sad state of affairs when so many people have to leave our country to buy medicine at an affordable rate.

Enough opining!

The vast majority of those responding to our survey, 82%, have been full-timing for less than 5 years. Almost 62% have been on the road full-time for 3 years or less. That leaves about 18% who have been living the good life for 5 years or more. No doubt there are many more long term full-timers out there. After all, full-time RVing is not new. Many people have laid the ground work for we rookies and we appreciate the large number of them that are willing to share their experiences. You can read all the books you want on the subject but the best way to learn about full-timing is to talk to those who have lived it.

On average people on the road full-time spend about 10 months out of the year traveling. It appears as though many of them hibernate for a few of the winter months in states like Arizona, California, Texas and Florida. When they do travel about 60% only stay for one week at a time in any one location. Obviously the length of time can vary depending upon their reason for visiting a certain community. Those that stay a month or more, about 33%, generally want to spend more time exploring the area, working a job, or just don't want to travel as much. Just over 7% spend more than six months at one location or as long as a job or circumstances require.

Our survey tells us that the average person travels about 13,000 miles per year with their RV. Some said they travel as much as 30,000 miles. Others travel only about 6,000 miles per year. The great thing about having a home on wheels is that you can determine how far you want to go, when you want to go and where you want to go.   It also gives you the option to pick up and move to another location if weather is turning bad, if a relative is driving you nuts or you just don't like your neighbor. We had an experience recently with hurricane Ophelia while we were visiting the North Carolina Coast. Before Ophelia arrived we packed up and moved 60 miles inland where we were safe and sound.

We were also curious about the number of people who might plan ahead and make reservations at RV parks either along the route they were traveling or at their destination. In talking with people we found that many of them like to go and take their chances. They tell us they have never had a problem finding a place to stay. We are a bit more anal about that and still tend to make reservations wherever we go. In fact the survey showed that approximately 57% of the folks out there do make reservations. That still leaves 43% with a true pioneer spirit.

Some people who full-time RV still have a place to call home as they own a house or in some cases own an RV lot at an RV Resort. Only 10% of the people we heard from still own a house. Many of them have it rented out. Approximately 13% own an RV lot. With an RV lot you can normally have a shed to store things. It also provides an affordable place to land for a while if you want to settle down for a few months. Generally you are only paying a monthly association fee and your electricity. Many of us still have a storage shed we use to store our favorite things because we still have that doubt as to whether or not we will want to continue the lifestyle and for how long. That is a natural reaction. The longer we are on the road the more comfortable we are with the lifestyle and the desire to remain full-time RVer's. However, we still find it difficult to think about getting rid of everything in our storage shed.

One big question we had is why did these people choose to change their lifestyle? Naturally the majority of the responding parties are retired or semi-retired. More interesting is the fact that a large number, 40%, went full-time because of their desire to travel. That is followed by 20% who did it to live more economically. Approximately 6% went full-time to accommodate their business and just fewer than 3% made the change in lifestyle to escape the stress of the working environment because of health concerns. Obviously many people were very happy to get out of their work environment and away from the day to day stresses. As a full-timer you can associate with people if you desire or become a hermit for a while if you need time to chill. Some comments on why people made the change were indicative of why most people choose full-timing. One person did it because his aunts and uncles were full-timers and they loved it. Other comments included: They just wanted a simpler lifestyle; Love it, can't imagine living in a stick house again; Tired of NY winters; Jobs; and the ability for both to retire early. Early retirement is a dream of most Americans and full-time RVing can make that dream come true.

So, once you make the decision to go out on the road how do you stay in touch with family, friends and your income sources? Technology has come a long way since many people started full-timing years ago. In fact we often wonder how people who did this 10 or 20 years ago managed to do some of the things that we do today. Talk about pioneer spirit, those folks certainly had an abundance of it. As you can probably guess a large number of people are communicating by cell phone and email. However, not all of them. There are still a few people who choose to use pay phones and snail mail. Some use a personal web site and a few use ham radios to communicate around the world. For the most part cell phone service is pretty good throughout the country. Later on we will talk about other ways to communicate. We will also talk about mail forwarding services which are vital to your ability to receive necessary mail such as license renewals. We have found that about 87% of full-timers use mail forwarding services. Others receive their mail through family members or others.

Receiving email can be challenging at times. We find that it takes a combination of services to allow us to connect wherever we are parked. Several people use a land line to connect to the internet. Others will use their cell phone or wi-fi cards. We find that a growing number of RV Parks are providing either free wi-fi or wi-fi at a low rate. Another method being used by about 20% of the road warriors is a PC Card provided by cell phone companies. There are however many other methods being used. They include Cyber café's, Kinko's, a Starband Mobile Flyer Dish, Library, Datastorm or Directway Satellite. The bottom line is that there is no reason a person cannot be connected. As time goes by methods of communication will be even more available and cost effective.

In later chapters we will cover other information provided to us by full-timers. This will include what type of RV's they are living in, how big and how old they are. We will also talk about places they like to visit, favorite places they like to eat and some of their favorite activities while traveling.

This is a very brief synopsis of who full-time RVers are. As you can see it is a booming lifestyle and we feel safe to say that it will only grow leaps and bounds as "Baby Boomers" near the end of their work years.

2 – IT'S NOT YOUR PARENTS CAMPING

Most of us have spent summer vacations and a few random weekends camping in a nearby state park. Often we hauled a station wagon load of equipment and supplies and spent a good deal of the time packing, setting up and later tearing down our "camp". We watched our parents cook dinner over a campfire or the always dependable Coleman stove. Many families still enjoy the great outdoors in this fashion. As we grew older we recreated this memorable experience with our children teaching them the value and joy of spending time outdoors.

There comes a point however when most of us grow weary of sleeping in musty sleeping bags on cold, lumpy and often damp tent floors. We long for accommodations that offer a few more creature comforts. It is at this point that many of us began our quest for the perfect "camping" experience. It is not until you graduate into a cab over camper, pop up trailer, travel trailer, 5th wheel or motor home that you begin to understand the difference between camping and RVing. RVing is generally defined by spending time in the great outdoors with clean hair, make up applied and feeling great after a good nights sleep. A hot shower, inside cooking and color TV are no longer options but rather requirements. You joke that your idea of "roughing it" means not having a dishwasher. RV'ers generally have coordinated dishes and tableware. They frequently use table cloths, placemats and decorations to adorn their dinning table. Kool Aid has been replaced by bottles of good wine along with a gourmet meal. At the risk of sounding snobbish, it is this type of life style that has fostered millions of people to move to full or part time RVing. The RV manufacturers realized that they had a gold mine and began improving the units they produced each year. Just like the new cars that hit the market each year, we are always looking for innovation and changes that offer us an RV that meets more of our needs and most closely resembles our stick homes. Storage has been improved dramatically as people voiced a desire to transport more and more of the items they have grown accustomed to using each day. Naturally you can have a custom RV designed and built to your specifications, that is if you have an unlimited supply of money. Little by little the more affordable RV's have included these previously unattainable features. Second bathrooms, second bedrooms and luxury kitchen features are now available in some types of RV's. The addition of "sliders" or as our parents called them; "tip outs" have made a huge impact in the market. They are so desirable that even cab over campers have slide outs now. We became really excited several years ago when we saw the first RV with "opposing slide outs" in the main living area. Upscale counter tops, ceiling fans and electronic equipment have made long term residence not only convenient, comfortable and affordable but desirable.

Remodeling and redecorating your RV to make it more "your home" is an option that not many people consider. Furniture, flooring, wall coverings and several other features can be changed to meet your needs and desires. We have altered many features in RV's we have owned. We pulled up the carpet and replaced it with a wood look vinyl floor covering. We pulled out a couch and built in a day bed type of structure covered with an upholstered pad. The area under the day bed became valuable storage and the bed actually was far more comfortable than the old hide-a-bed we removed. We have re-papered walls and put up new borders. In one rather wild move we painted the patterned bumper that surrounded our bed. By combining regular craft paint with an additive to make it suitable for fabric, we painted it a neutral color that coordinated with the wall covering. This allowed us to use patterned bedspreads and change them at will.

The important message here is that you are restricted only by the extent of your imagination. In the first stages of our RVing we purchased a very used and dated class C RV. We changed many things in that old clunker including the counter tops. They were not only ugly, but had stains and burns. We purchased a covering that came in a roll and you cut it to fit. Using a household iron, you affixed it right to the old top with heat. It looked great for a very long time. This same unit had an unattractive color stripe on the outside and we quickly fixed that with some creative spray painting.

Personalizing your new home is another very important yet complicated prospect. Everything you add to your RV must be analyzed for storage and portability. We actually have a gallery of family pictures in our bedroom. We also hung many other pictures from our home that we had grown very fond of. We use a picture hanging kit that has a wire that hangs from a tight clip. They come in the inexpensive kits you can pick up at most stores, even grocery stores. Please use extra caution when thinking about using any type of nail or screw in your walls. You should be certain that it is in a safe area where there are no wires, etc. We use crafters clay on each lower corner and that keeps our precious pictures still while traveling and as a great side effect, they stay level! The clay is generally safe on walls and won't pull the paper off nor stain it. Naturally you can use the extra strong Velcro type tape as well. The reason we chose the first method is to allow us the option of changing pictures as we wanted to. The sit around items are a bit more challenging. We have seen folks who actually affix sit around items to counters and shelves in a semi permanent fashion. This little trick was shared with us by folks from Southern California who were accustomed to earth quake activity. If your RV doesn't have space for this luxury, you will want to select special items that can be secured without too much fuss. I wrap a couple of items in a dish towel and place them in one of the chairs.

Furniture is another item that we have found people customize to meet their own needs. Many RV's now come with the option of a free standing dinning room table and chairs. It is not uncommon for people to request that the old favorite booth be removed or not installed in the first place. A more traditional dinning room table and chairs can be substituted if you desire. It is important to mention that the booth does offer large storage drawers and that is valuable space you will want to think about loosing before taking it out. We have remodeled the furniture in several units and currently are enjoying two big recliners instead of the traditional couch. We added a beautiful desk and small dinette set. Naturally you must give much thought as to how you will secure these pieces for travel as the furniture the RV comes equipped with is generally locked in place with large bolts. You should talk to your RV dealer or the RV manufacturer about ways to secure your furniture.

Many of us have become accustomed to decorating for the holidays and struggle with taking these items along with us. We selected a few lightweight and unbreakable items for each holiday and packed them into one of those wonderful big plastic tubs. This allows us to decorate and avoid that home sickness that overcomes some folks. Most people use strings of lights to decorate and you will find they are available in almost any style you can imagine.

One hint is that most of the string lights are made the same. The decorative light covers pop on and off without much effort. You could easily carry a couple of strings of lights and several different covers that you change as your mood changes. This maximizes your storage space. The rope lights have become increasingly popular recently and we see them in quite a variety of colors and placement. It is fun to wrap trees in areas you are spending a bit more time. Another popular option is to outline your patio space outside. It gives a festive look to your little space and actually serves to guide you when are walking at night. Still popular are the colorful and expressive wind socks and flags we have grown to love. Once again, let your imagination be your guide. This is your home and you should make it reflect your personality.

Many people are very fond of their gardens and plants. One friend told me over and over that she didn't think she could live without her dirt to dig in. They now have a handful of hardy plants that they put in plastic bins in their shower for travel. Upon arrival she sets them outside to soak up the sunshine. She tells me she now has the best of both worlds.

"What is it, how much does it weigh and why do we need it?" This was our chant for a long time as we picked the things we would add to our new home. Another was "If I can't wear it, eat it or spend it, I don't want it." This was repeated to our friends and family for many months prior

to "hitting the road? We realized that we had to be very
selective when making choices and after a bit of thought
the children found they could still gift us and not break the
scale. Gift cards are a great option you can offer them.
We especially like gift cards to restaurants and on-line
shopping sites.

Your choice of RV will depend on funds available, planned
use and naturally your personal taste. The RV we
purchased specifically to begin our full-time adventure was
one we looked at for over a year. We finally decided that it
had the necessary "AH" factor. Each time we went back to
look at it, we both exclaimed "AH" this is what we were
looking for.

Your needs and desires may change as you go through
your adventure. It is easy to meet people who swear by a
specific type of unit. Their reasons are generally very
personal with a bit of economic consideration thrown in.

We touched on the aspect of cooking and how different RV
cooking is from tent camping. It is not to say that you
won't want to occasionally cook outside but more often
than not, you will be using a BBQ not a camp stove. In the
early years we would prepare meals in advance to
minimize the amount of time and energy needed while out.
As we moved ahead into larger, better appointed RV's we
began actually cooking more complicated dishes and
menus as we had more time to spend on a beautiful
dinner, sometimes even by candle light. For the serious

cook, there is little that you won't be able to create in your new home. Many RVers enjoy visiting specific areas as berries and other fall goodies are ready for harvest. They actually can or freeze jams, jellies and other delicacies. Several couples that we have met have devoted precious storage space to a small freezer. A freezer allows them the luxury of freezing fresh fish that they have caught as well as other edible treasures you find along your way. Naturally it also allows you to take advantage of sales on your favorite food items as well.

Many RV's in the past few years have stopped coming equipped with the traditional oven. This has been replaced with a combination convection oven / microwave unit mounted over the stovetop. For the person without experience with convection cooking it takes practice to perfect this type of baking. It is a bit scary at first and we recommend that you select something very easy to start out. In general we find that when using our convection oven we must add time to the cooking cycle to achieve the same results we are accustomed to. The combination option allows you to speed up the process somewhat. Some models of the combination oven allow for broiling and some do not. Ours did not so we opted for a toaster oven that we can use for toast and broiling small items. Read your users manual carefully and give it a try. Most people we talk with love the newer way to bake and are happy to have the additional space left vacant by the old oven. One couple we met even had a dishwasher installed in the space they had after removing the oven.

The showers and commodes have come a long way. Most have porcelain toilets and some even have custom seats. The showers most often have skylights and are large and roomy. Some even have seats in the shower to make personal care easier.

Another improvement is in the quality of the mattress in a newer RV. Many come standard with a Sleep Number bed or name brand mattress. It is not a problem however to change a mattress. You must take measurements with you to make a purchase, but the sizes are not far off. Most people do not use both mattress and box springs but this is actually more an issue of personal choice and space than anything else. You must measure and plan for this change. Not all stores will sell just the mattress, some sell only in sets. Personally we chose to purchase a sleep number bed that actually gave us a bit more width. To support this we simply used plywood on top of the original support. The pump fits in the under bed storage and we drilled holes for the tubes that take air from the pump to the mattress and it works beautifully. One added bonus we found was that we reduced weight with this type of set up. More and more of the high end RV's now are sporting this same type of mattress as a standard feature. We were also pleased to learn that adding this new base does not affect our ability to lift the bed for access to the under bed storage. We do have one tip to pass on, when traveling through changing altitudes, your air bed may inflate. We suggest that you reduce the air in the mattress before heading out and adjust it at bedtime.

Your choice of dishes and cooking pans is a very personal one. Plastic and Corelle are safe but we suggest that you incorporate some things you would have in your stick home. The advent of bubble wrap and non skid rubber mats have made it much easier to have those breakable items that make your RV more like home. We had a glass of wine with a wonderful couple we met in Florida and got a kick when she pulled out beautiful crystal wine glasses that she transported in their own "socks". The socks were indeed thick sports stockings that they had purchased and just pulled over their beautiful stemware. It is important to be cautious and not put too many heavy items in your cupboards. We have settled on a bit of a mix and find it perfect. One secret is to be sure to either fill the space or pad it to avoid things from banging against each other. We have a small liquor cabinet and put a little couch pillow in with the bottles before driving away. The expandable bars you can purchase at any RV store and at most department stores help to secure cupboards as well.

How do you deal with your laundry is another question we are asked frequently. We chose to have a washer dryer combination unit in our RV. We began by making a costly mistake when we purchased a non-vented unit. The size of the load was tiny and it took 3 to 4 hours to complete the wash-dry process. After the long wait for a load of laundry to complete, we found the clothes so wrinkled that you had to iron almost everything. Our interest was to have the ability to do at least part of our laundry in the RV, we went to a vented version of the same type of unit. The difference is amazing. Additionally, the size of a load is slightly larger and clothes come out less wrinkled. We still press a few things, but not everything. We use commercial laundry facilities on occasion for larger items like bed spreads or large throw rugs and when we are paying for electricity although we have found that is does not cost any more to wash a load in the motor home than it does to take it to a laundry mat. A good friend of ours washes his clothes in his RV and then takes them to the laundry for drying. We met one couple who had a closet converted to accommodate an apartment style stacking washer dryer unit. It is large and will do almost everything.

A word of caution is warranted at this point regarding purchasing items for your RV from specialty stores only. In all fairness, there are some things you will find only at an RV supply store but there are many things that work just as well that you can purchase at a regular store and at a much more reasonable price. You will want to think through a purchase before paying the inflated prices at some RV stores.

3 – WHAT TYPE OF RV WILL WORK FOR YOU?

In the previous chapter we talked about amenities that are available to make life comfortable on the road. To reiterate, today's full-timers are not campers we are RVer's. Although we may stay in some of the same parks as campers there is a distinct difference in how we live our daily lives and how people who are on a weekend camping trip enjoy their time out in the wilderness. Don't forget, full-time RVing is not necessarily a vacation, it is a lifestyle. Although to some it may seem like a permanent vacation. When you visit RV sales lots and see the types of RV's available today you will realize what we mean. RV's of today are much more spacious, have all the amenities and make for very comfortable living quarters. Not your typical camper. In fact our children laughed when we first bought our 5th wheel and we went "camping" prior to going full-time. They said "This is not camping" and they were right. We are not just talking about the million dollar RV's you see on the Travel Channel. This includes many affordable trailers, 5th wheels, class C Motor Homes and Class A Motor Homes. True, RV's are not as spacious as your stick home but to put things in perspective think about those who live in small 250 square foot apartments in NYC. The space in your RV will feel like a mansion compared to that.

What should you look for when thinking about living full-time in your RV? There are many books available on how to find the right one for you. We recommend that you do your research and talk to sales people and RV owners to get a sense of what other people are saying. We cannot emphasize enough the point that we made in the first chapter, talk to as many people as you can. No one has all the answers. The lifestyle you live and the RV you buy should be what you are comfortable with. Remember the "AH" factor. If you walk into an RV and it feels good it probably is the one for you. We suggest however that you take your time and see other units prior to committing to the one that gave you the "AH" emotion. Then go back to that one and if you have the same reaction then you should give it some serious thought. One major argument that you will hear often is whether it is better to own a Diesel or a gas motor home. There are many pros and cons but the bottom line is what works best for you and what you can afford. We also suggest you visit on-line forums and maybe even ask some questions yourself. Forums such as Fulltime RVer (ftrv.com), campingworld.com under resources, rv.net, and woodalls.com, to name a few, would give you ample opportunity to find answers too many of your questions and also allow you to ask questions. Please be aware that as you read these forums you will run into people who will have their own agenda, are on a soapbox trying to convince everyone that certain vehicles are absolutely terrible or, that you would be nuts if you don't do something the way they say to do it. That is not to say that you won't get a ton of outstanding advice. There are a lot of people who truly want to help.

To give you an example of the rigs that might be out on the road we would like to refer back to the non-scientific survey that we talked about in the first chapter. We asked people to tell us what type of RV they are living in, what length it is and the age of the vehicle.

Just over 51% of our respondents are living in Class A Motor Homes. The average length is 38 feet and the average age is around 3.8 years.

Next in line is 5th Wheel travel trailers sometimes referred to as 5ers. Around 39% were living in 5th wheels with an average length of 36 feet and an average age of 4.7 years.

This is followed by Class C Motor Homes. Almost 8% of the respondents are living in Class C's with an average length of 29 feet and an average age of 4.5 years. It is amazing what they are doing with Class C Motor Homes these days. Some of them are as nice and as well equipped as some Class A's.

The final vehicle of choice is Travel Trailers. Just over 2% live in travel trailers with and average length of 20 feet and an average age of 13 years. We know this one is most likely not correct as there are probably a lot more people out there in newer, longer, travel trailers with slide-outs.

That being said we believe that the preponderance of full-timers are either living in Class A Motor Homes or 5th Wheel Trailers. Size and comfort most likely have a lot to do with it.

Again, what works for one person is not necessarily what is right for another person. Do you have a fear of driving a big motor home? Although they are relatively easy to manipulate they do take some time to learn how to drive. You might be more comfortable with a truck pulling a trailer or a 5th wheel. Keep in mind that trailers tend to sway a little more in the wind than 5th wheels. We were very happy pulling a 5th wheel. It had triple axels and seldom swayed in the wind. The main difficulty with trailers and 5th wheels is backing them into a spot. Many RV parks today have pull-through sites which allow you to pull straight in without having to back up. We suggest that this is the best way to go if at all possible. If you've never backed a trailer longer than 10 feet or have never backed one up at all, we highly recommend you practice, practice, practice. Do this not only for safety and protection of your equipment but to save a lot of frustration and embarrassment. We've all been there when someone comes into a park and spends an hour trying to back into a spot. It is embarrassing, frustrating and causes us to use words we normally would not use. How do we know? "Been there done that." That is not to say that motor homes cannot be difficult to back as well. You should practice with your motor home so you feel comfortable with it. We have found however that having a backup camera and audio on the back of the motor home to give verbal instructions has made life a lot easier for us. Backing into a spot and navigating are two things that can cause great tension in a relationship. When you are living together 24/7 you want to avoid as many tension related events as possible. GPS and backup cameras tend to make life more bearable for everyone. We have also found that simple walkie-talkies work well to communicate with the driver. In addition you should take time learn some basic signals and be consistent with them.

You should also consider what length RV you can handle plus where you will be going with that RV. Driving or pulling a big, long, RV can be scary and takes a lot of practice in turning, etc. Once you decide what length you think you can handle then consider where you might visit with the RV. If you plan to visit mostly state or federal parks you need to be aware that there are size limitations at many of these parks. Some allow only RVs as small as 20 feet others around 30 feet. So if you going to visit parks we suggest a smaller RV. Most RV parks can handle just about any size RV. Be sure to check with the park about their size limitations before you get somewhere and find that you cannot get in because you are too big.

There are also physical aspects of set up that you need to consider. For us it has been somewhat easier to set up a motor home than a trailer or 5th wheel. Again it depends on the individual. If you have back problems or other physical limitations you might want to consider a motor home. Disconnecting a hitch and manually lowering stabilizers can be a bit challenging at times.

You must also consider what you will use for transportation once you are set up. If you are pulling a trailer or 5th wheel you obviously have a vehicle to use to tour the area once you disconnect. However, some of the larger trucks do have difficulty traversing areas with narrow streets and limited parking. If you have a motor home you will be limited to using public transportation or to the use of your motor home to see the sights unless you tow a vehicle. We have seen various types of towing from a complete trailer with the car loaded on it to tow bars used to connect the car to the motor home. Towing a car will provide you with a more economical way to see the sights and save you some hassle by not having to continuously set up and strike your motor home to use it for sightseeing. There are a few things you should be aware of prior to buying a vehicle to tow. Check state laws to make sure you are following the law with regard to weight limits, etc. Also check with your motor home manufacturer to determine how much weight your motor home can handle. Make sure the car is towable. The ideal situation is to have a vehicle that, when towed, does not register mileage. If you're using a dolly or a full trailer this is generally not a problem.

However, if you are towing with all four wheels on the ground you need make sure your vehicle is set up to disconnect the odometer while being towed. There are many manufacturers that provide this option. Check with your motor home dealer and do some on-line research to make sure you have a vehicle that can be towed with all four wheels on the ground. If not then you would need to use the option of a dolly or a trailer. We tow a 1999 Saturn that has worked very well for us. We suggest you visit web sites such as trailerlife.com, campingworld.com and motorhomemagazine.com to learn more about towing a vehicle. We need to make one final comment about towing a vehicle. We cannot over emphasize the need to use a braking system on the vehicle being towed. They might seem a bit expensive but they pale in comparison to burning out your motor home brake system or losing control while going down a steep hill. No matter how small the vehicle, they do push on the motor home and can cause problems when trying to slow down or stop. This is one area you should not skimp on. Besides many states have laws requiring brake systems.

Because there are hundreds of RV options available to you we will not go into what make or model we think would be best for you. Just take your time, talk to people, do your research, look at several models, and remember the "AH" Factor.

4 – SO YOU THINK YOU WANT TO DO THIS?   HERE ARE A FEW THINGS TO CONSIDER

- ❖ Planning

- ❖ Communication

- ❖ Health and Dental Insurance and medications

- ❖ Finding medical care

- ❖ Telling Family and Friends

- ❖ Registration of vehicles

- ❖ Storing your treasures

- ❖ Budget

- ❖ Park discount plans and memberships

- ❖ Extra charges

- ❖ Record Keeping

- ❖ Newsletter

- ❖ Shopping

- ❖ Hair care

- ❖ Pets

- ❖ Pet care and grooming

- ❖ GPS

- ❖ Mail forwarding service

Planning

There is no substitute for planning. It is wise to plan for several different scenarios. These vary greatly depending upon different situations. Some things are mandatory like income resources, health insurance and if you will keep a stick home. The other topics are very important as well, but may or may not alter your decision as dramatically.

The following is a description of things you need to consider as you move through the planning process.

Communication

Gone are the days when traveling this wonderful country of ours meant you would be out of touch with friends and family. This can be arranged for in a wide variety of ways. Some do quite well finding pay phones and using them to maintain contact with family, friends and business associates. You can use cash, a phone card or purchase calling cards to make land line calls, however it is generally difficult for them to contact you. There are several new ways to maintain the level of communication you have grown accustomed to.   Some RV'ers that stay for longer periods (2 to 6 months) in one park will choose to have a phone line installed at their site. Indeed most new RV's are equipped with a regular telephone and are pre-wired for a land line.   Many parks have the wiring already in place at the sites. The RV'er will contact the local telephone company to arrange service.

Cell phones are now available at very affordable rates and coverage improves every day. Some people who plan to spend a lot of time in very remote locations have chosen to purchase satellite phones. They are more expensive to purchase and the minute charge is rather high. Note: the cost of satellite equipment and service are coming down as time goes by which warrants checking it out. More often than not, the person who spends a large amount of time traveling or is a full-timer will choose a combination approach. As Cell phone coverage has increased and internet service is available through several methods, most have made the step up to the wireless technology.
Internet is now available via PC card, Wi-fi connections, satellite communications systems and remote modem locations. Personally we compared the service of several cell phone carriers. We chose Verizon for both cell and Internet Connection. We chose a plan with a lot of minutes per month to assure that we could have long talks with our family and friends as well as business associates. You will want to consider a plan that does not charge for roaming, as you will rarely be using the phone within the assigned area code. Additionally, some carriers offer plans that allow you to talk unlimited minutes with other subscribers without charging minutes. For internet connection we chose a PC card plan with 24/7 coverage as well. We have not regretted these expenses. It is a great comfort to have your cell near you at all times. If someone needs you quickly, they generally have instant access. If you refer

back to chapter 2 additional communications options are listed.

Health Insurance

This is a tough one for the not yet eligible for Medicare folks. We did a lot of research and found that most plans were either out of our budget (by a lot) or they wouldn't provide coverage because of pre-existing conditions. We found an organization for the self-employed (NASE). They offer insurance through Mega Life. We then learned that some states have passed laws forbidding insurance companies from rating or declining coverage for anyone. You will need to be legal residents of the state you purchase health insurance in. It is important to research several different plans well in advance of your target date to avoid a lapse in coverage. A lapse in coverage may disallow you coverage based on the Federal Portability Act. Prescription plans are an important component to any policy you consider. Naturally, the number of medications a person needs will vary and will be subject to change at any time. Most policies have a maximum annual benefit for prescriptions. Often there is an annual deductible as well. After meeting your deductible for the year, the full cost of a prescription will be deducted from the annual cap amount. You may only pay a co-payment, but the insurance company will tally the full fee that they pay the pharmacy. Example: you are given a prescription for an antibiotic. The pharmacy sells that medication for $100.

You have the prescription filled and pay the pharmacy a $10.00 co-payment. The pharmacy bills your insurance company $90 which is the amount they charge for the medication minus the co-payment you paid. The insurance company charges your account $90.00 toward your annual maximum. As you can see, it doesn't take long for someone on monthly medications to use their allowance rather quickly. Be sure to research the policy specifics carefully as they vary greatly.

There are a couple of ways to work through this dilemma. If any of your medications are available in generic form and your doctor approves this form of the medication, it may be advantageous to purchase them outright for cash (not running it through your insurance company) from a large chain pharmacy such as Costco, Sam's Club or Wal*Mart. Determining the financial viability of purchasing your medications is as simple as phoning the pharmacy and giving them the details of your prescription. Ask them what they would charge for larger quantities such as 3, 6 or 12 months at a time. Naturally if you are considering this option, you will want to explain it to your physician and gain their approval for larger quantities. Most physicians are accustomed to dispensing medications in quantities that cover one month at a time. Some physicians require office visits on a regular basis before dispensing medications. You will need to talk to your physician before you proceed. Not all medications can be dispensed this way. If you choose to purchase the prescription and pay cash you may find that you actually pay less than your co-payment would have been and you will reserve the annual amount for emergencies and medication changes that you didn't plan for.

Another option that is becoming more and more popular is purchasing your medications in either Mexico or Canada. There are skeptics who do not believe that the quality of these medications is acceptable, but there are millions of Americans who routinely purchase their medications this way. (Consumers should be aware that the federal government has taken the position that the importation of certain drugs from outside of the U.S. may violate federal law.) If you are able to take generic brands you can save a great deal of money. Mexico will sell you almost any medication you need with a few exceptions. They will not sell controlled substances without a prescription from a physician with a Mexican Medical license. Controlled substances are things like pain medications (Hydrocodone, Vicodin, Oxycodone and the like). They won't sell you sleeping pills or sedatives (also known as tranqulizers) such as Valium and Zanax.

It is very important to note that the Mexican Government has very little tolerance of people attempting to purchase controlled drugs. They have in fact arrested and jailed people for this practice.

They may not have the newest medications and unusual medications such as chemotherapy and transplant (anti-rejection) medications are not generally available. Routine medications such as cholesterol lowering, hypertension controllers, hormones and antibiotics are available without prescription. Be sure that you take the details of your prescription with you to insure you buy the right strength and quantity. The clerks in the Mexican pharmacies are very helpful and will really go out of their way to help you. Be cautious and verify that the medication they offer you is indeed the same as the one you are taking in the US. You may request or will be offered medications that are purchased in the US and are packaged in English and will be familiar to you. They will also offer, at a much reduced cost, the Mexican version and the packaging is in Spanish. If you have any reservations about the Mexican version of your medication it is best to pay the difference for the US version. You should check with current US Customs regulations regarding quantity prior to purchasing medications abroad. You should be able to purchase a good supply during any one trip. You need not be concerned about having Mexican currency for your purchases. They are happy to accept US dollars and also have the ability to charge a credit card if you so desire. Medications may also be purchased in Canada however you will need to have a prescription from your US physician before they will sell to you. Additionally some Canadian pharmacies are still selling prescriptions over the internet.

It is advisable to research and compare all the options and to consult with your physician before choosing one of the unconventional options.

Dental Care

Many US citizens go to Mexico specifically to have dental work done. There are many Mexican Dentists who are available within walking distance of the borders. There are several small communities that exist solely to sell medications and provide medical and dental services to US citizens. Some of the Doctors and Dentists will even complete your insurance claim forms for you. It is advisable to procure a referral from a friend or someone who has actually used a specific dentist or physician.

A Mexican Dentist will give you an estimate of charges for the work you request. They will want to be paid in cash and will give you a receipt that you may be able to use toward your US tax liability. Check with your tax accountant to determine what tax deductions are allowed. The quality of the dental work is generally excellent. Naturally there may well be dentists who do not meet the standard US citizens have grown accustomed to but there are always those exceptions. The majority of their business is fostered by word of mouth and if they do not perform quality work, the patient will spread the word and that could severely inhibit their ability to make a living.

For the most part the fees they charge are about 1/3 of the fees charged by Dentists in the US.

Mexican dentists and their staffs speak English. In some cases the English of the staff is not as fluent as the doctor. Our experience is in a little border town outside of Yuma, AZ. The village of Los Algodones exists as a convenient location for US citizens to find medical, dental, optical, prescription, cigarettes, liquor and other Mexican treasures. We have found our trips to this wonderful little village to be a lot of fun and look forward to returning there each year as we "winter" in Yuma.

When going into Mexico to have work done you should be aware that the Mexican citizens function with a different understanding of time than Americans do. They will schedule an appointment for you and will begin your work near to that time, but frequently they will work at a much slower pace than you have grown accustomed to. Take something to keep you busy like a book or other busy work. It is not uncommon for you to spend most of the day in and out of the dental chair. Additionally you should bring a large supply of patience with you to the appointment, you will need it! The quality of their work and attention to detail is exceptional. A personal experience involved some cosmetic work. The dentist was so concerned about absolute perfection that he had the technician from the lab come to his office to see just how the cap looked next to my other teeth.

The other services available in Mexico are vision care, hearing aids and several alternative medicine treatments for serious ailments such as cancer.

The Mexican government takes your safety very seriously. They have an entire arm of their police force that is devoted entirely to the safety of the tourist. Naturally your level of comfort is very personal and if you have reservations about going into a foreign country, the above mentioned opportunities may not be for you. We recommend that you speak to others who have traveled to Mexico about the specifics of entry and expected behaviors in the area where you will cross the border. The people in your RV park can also provide a wealth of knowledge on these subjects. The people you meet are generally more than happy to share experiences and give you recommendations on any of these subjects.

Finding medical care on the road

The reduced stress lifestyle of RVing is without argument good for your health; however we are all subject to unexpected health problems. It is important to know what you would do in the event of an emergency as well as a less urgent illness. Most RV parks give you a pamphlet or sheet of information that tells you who and how to contact someone for help. Almost all areas use the generic 911 system to summon help in an emergency. It is advisable to keep this paperwork handy so that you can refer to it in a hurry. If you summon an ambulance, you will need to tell them your park site # so that they may find you quickly. Some of the larger parks have a security person that should be notified when possible. This allows security to quickly lead the rescue vehicles to your site.

In the event of a non-emergency health problem you should identify a local and hopefully close by urgent or ambulatory care center. You can always go to the local emergency room, but be aware that the fees charged are much higher and some health insurances will not pay your claim in full as they require life threatening illness and injuries for emergency room / department treatment. It is wise to inquire when you register at a new park as to the location of Urgent care centers and hospitals. We learned this valuable lesson when we arrived in a new city on a weekend. Tom was extremely sick and had been home medicating for an upper respiratory infection, and he was loosing the battle. After driving around for over an hour, we were unable to locate an urgent care center finally went to the local hospital. It was quite a surprise when we got the bill in the mail. The fee was 3 to 4 times that which we would have expected at an urgent care. We continue to be amazed when RV parks do not routinely include this information in their registration packets. Ask for it, maybe they will get the message!

Telling the children, family and friends

Another big obstacle to overcome is telling your children, family and friends. It most likely won't come as a big surprise to them as you most likely have been talking about this lifestyle for a long time. It is beneficial to have your target date selected when you tell them of your plans. Some families are skeptical about this lifestyle and will only feel better when you have taken the time to explain to them how it will work. It is important to tell them the ways you plan to maintain communication. They will be more comfortable if you can give them a tentative itinerary as well. If your family is spread out over the country, you will be able to show them how frequently you will be able to visit. Many RVers tell us they are able to see their families much more frequently in their new lifestyle.   In the case of the younger children (Grand children) there are many creative ways you can stay in touch. You can do such fun things as mailing the children pieces of a map as you travel to the different states. This allows them to track your trip in a visual way. Some people use a cassette recorder and send the children tapes describing their adventures. Yet another couple told us that they buy and mail home Tee shirts from most of the areas they visit. The children don't forget and are quick to remind them of changing sizes. There are no limits on how to stay in touch with the little ones except your imagination.

Technology has once again come to our rescue. The computer allows for frequent emailing as well as instant messaging. Web cams have become affordable and are a great gift for the people you want to see frequently. We gifted our children and one married grand daughter with web cameras before starting our most recent big trip. Now we book Web Cam time and it has kept the homesickness bug at bay on many an occasion. A digital camera is also a blessing. We email our family pictures of special things as they do us. We recently welcomed a new family member, a beautiful Great Granddaughter. We received emailed pictures taken with her grandpa's cell phone within minutes after she was born. It really took the sting out of not being there for the birth.

What do we do with all our treasures?

If you choose to sell your home and live in your RV full-time you will have to make a decision about what to do with all your possessions. There are several options to choose from depending on your plans. On a personal note, when we told our children we also told them that we were selling our house and that we wanted to know which of our things they wanted. Their first reaction was that they didn't want any of our treasures; they had enough of their own. Well, they soon changed their minds about all that! We actually had a big family day where they took sticky notes with their names on them and put them on things they wanted. Funny how much they actually took in the end. The joy of that is that when we visit them, we see much of our old "stuff."

We then decided which things we wanted to put into storage and how we would store them. We literally went room by room and listed items in a category, sell, keep, give away, donate, put in RV or just throw away.   The choices on just how to store our remaining treasures were few. Our children didn't have the space to store it for us and that left only a commercial storage facility. We settled on purchasing a pre built wooden storage shed and placing it on our son's property. This way we were able to offer them the shed after we are through with it. The cost of a delivered pre-built wooden building was about the same as a storage facility would have been for a year.

Treasure Sale

There are a couple of ways to deal with the possessions that you are not keeping or giving away. Garage sales and auctions are just two. The length and frequency of either type of liquidation will depend on the number of items as well as the amount of time you have available. Some people choose to hold sales for several weekends to allow for the maximum return on their effort. The donation of items that you can't or don't want to sell is always a good option. One bit of advice is to pre-arrange for pick up at the end of the day of your sale or the next day. If you wait to call after the sale you may find yourself stuck with a driveway full of items that didn't sell. There are also some agencies that won't take everything you have left over. We made this mistake and were left with a driveway full of boxes awaiting someone to come haul them away for several days.   *Remember to get a receipt from the agency to use as a deduction on your taxes.

Budget

Once you establish a plan for your income, however large or small it is you must develop a budget. It will help you a lot when you realize that your expenses will be so much less than you are accustomed to spending each month. * We will give you a work sheet to help you develop a budget. For the most part the number of expenses you will have to deal with on a monthly basis will go down as you no longer have to pay for the usual expenses associated with a home. There are however a few things you might not have had in the past. Take a look at the work sheet and customize it for yourself.

RV Park clubs and discount programs

When the time comes to hit the road most of us need a travel plan. Most plans include making reservations for someplace to spend the night and for destinations. There are however, people who actually decide on a final destination and just get in the RV and start driving until they are tired or find a place to stop. If you have a strong enough sense of adventure this might be for you. There are many states that allow overnight stays in the rest stops. Some Wal*Marts and Flying J truck stops welcome overnight stays as well. Some Wal*Marts reportedly have been known to bring you a hot cup of coffee and a newspaper in the morning.   You can purchase an Atlas from Wal*Mart that includes a listing of store locations along with the usual maps and other interesting information. Note: some cities have ordinances against overnight parking even in private lots. Pay attention to signs in the parking lots.

For those of you who are not quite so adventurous you might want to plan a bit more. Most people have an idea of how many miles they want to travel in a day. Personally we try to limit our distance to 300 to 350 miles in a day. Leaving at a reasonable time in the morning gets us into a new stopping place around 3 or 3:30. That allows us plenty of time to relax do a few chores (like a load of laundry or a trip to the grocery store) before we head to bed. Naturally this will vary depending on personal choice and if you have more than one person to take the wheel or make lengthy stops along the way. We should mention that you will want to confirm arrival time with a new park as some actually charge a nominal fee if you arrive before a certain time. Armed with this information and a map you can determine a stop over location. From there you can use one or more methods of finding a park or stopping place. You can research the area via the internet by searching for RV parks in a specific area. You can refer to directories that you purchase like Trailer life's CD, AAA or other directories you purchase. There are also many membership programs you can join. They will provide you with a book with all the information and directions you will need. Some are rather expensive and some are more reasonable. Coast to Coast, RPI, and Thousand Trails are some of the big ones. They all require a rather sizable investment to buy in. In some cases you can buy a plan someone else wants to get out of. You can even find a time when they are running specials. Thousand Trails has an annual fee after the original price, but the camping is free. They limit your stay to two weeks at a time at any one park. Coast to Coast is not as expensive but does have an annual fee, and charges $8.00 to $13.00 per night for stays. Length of stay limits apply here too. Most of these parks are "destination Parks". That means they are most often off the beaten path, are large and have tons of activities available. Often they are not the best choice for overnight stays as you can log quite a few miles and waste time driving off the highway to reach them.

Passport America is a program sponsored by Camping World. They have a small ($44.) annual fee and you can stay at ½ the usual fee. They have a very large list of participating parks that is particularly easy to read. We find most serious RV'ers use this plan frequently. It is important to read the directory carefully as many of the parks limit the number of nights you can use the discount and the discount is not always available depending on the time of the year and local special events.

Good Sam is another one that has a small annual fee. The discount is usually 10 to 15 percent.

KOA parks are often some of the nicest parks across the country. They have an annual fee in the range of $15.00. They are franchised and for the most part very modern and clean. They are generally located in very convenient locations. They are however, also one of the most expensive.

If you plan to stay for longer periods of time many parks offer reduced rates for weekly and monthly stays. Also, as in most types of resort stays, the time of year will affect the rate. When making reservations be sure to ask about other discounts. Senior rates, AAA and other club discounts may help to keep you expenses down.

Many RV parks now have the option of making your reservation on line. You enter the specifics and receive an emailed confirmation right away. Some of the membership plans require that you purchase a block of points prior to booking a reservation. You can generally check the number of points you have available in your account through their Web site.

A final word on finding RV Parks. You can gain a wealth of information from the people you meet along the way. Most folks will ask where you are heading as a general question when you first meet. RV'ers are more than happy to share experiences about the good places as well as advice about the not so good places.

Extra charges

Many parks are adding additional fees when you use a discount plan. For example, additional fees may be charged for 50 amp service instead of 30, over 2 people staying, pets, air conditioning, cable service, and Wi-fi use. Some parks also charge you for electricity. We find this most often when staying a month or more at one time. Most parks have a change in their rates based on the time of the year. Example Arizona, Florida, Georgia, Texas, California and other southern states charge more for winter months and less for summer months due to warm weather periods. Ask about this change of rate if you think you are overlapping a seasonal change. They seem to vary depending on the park and the region. Additionally they frequently will have a cancellation fee, even if you give them a lot of notice. I have developed a list of questions that we ask with each reservation. * We will provide this list. You may want to add questions that are important to you.

Record keeping

It is a good idea to create a file to keep information you find about areas. You can clip magazine articles and save scraps of paper with the information you find in a geographic type of file. We set up an expanding type of file and use the alphabet tabs to correspond with the state the information is located in. You will also want to keep a log of parks you stay in. It allows you to avoid making a mistake twice. If you are computer literate and have the skill to set up a excel type of folder, you can keep the important information by date. We also use a file where we list the parks and details about the park. Remarks such things as Great pool, heated" or "near water".

We have an excel file that tracks our itinerary. We email it to our family and friends. It includes information about the reservation and also a telephone number for the park. This way if someone wants to contact us and is having trouble reaching us, they can leave a message with the park office. Additionally, this allows you to copy all or part of it and get it to friends and relatives who want to track your travels.

We purchased a binder type of folder with several pocket sections. We keep the most recent version of our itinerary in the front. We then keep reservation information such as emailed confirmations, directions or other printed information on the parks. This is great especially when you have made reservations quite a bit in advance. You won't be frantically searching for the information. We take this folder into the park office when we go in to register upon arrival. It helps us to know if we owe more money, to verify that the fee we are paying is what we agreed upon. * note, some parks quote you the rate including taxes and others don't. You may want to add that to the information you collect when you are making the reservation. We also keep copies of the dogs vaccination documents there as well, as some parks are requiring that you present proof of their vaccinations upon registration. Don't forget to take your membership card when using a discount plan. We have included a page that lists the make, model and year of the motor home and car. We also have the license plate information there too. Most parks want this information upon registration. We have also started giving the park our cell phone numbers in the event they need to get in touch with us while we are away from the park. We frequently find that making reservations can take a lot of time. We try never to call late in the day, as that is the time most parks are checking people in. We usually avoid Fridays and the weekends as well.

One thing you should consider is the purchase of a portable safe. You will want to keep important papers such as birth certificates, pass ports, insurance papers and anything else that would be difficult to replace. Naturally this is a good place to keep your good jewelry. They are available in a huge variety of sizes and price ranges. They can be found in most of the large chain superstores as well as Home Depot and Lowe's. You will want to pick one that is easily carried and yet will hold your valuables. They come rated for the heat that they will withstand. This is of course very important in the event of a fire.

News Letter

Many RV'ers write a newsletter and send it out to select friends and relatives. It can be sent via Internet or in printed form. Personally we have been doing this since we began our adventure. At first we didn't know if people really read it. At one point we ran a bit longer than usual between issues and were very surprised when several people contacted us and wanted to know where their newsletter was. They told us how much they looked forward to receiving it and reading about our latest escapades. Some tell us they are living our adventure vicariously through our newsletter.

Shopping

Anyone who is just starting out in this type of adventure either full or part time will undergo a re-education on how to do many things, including shopping. Many of the rules you lived by for so many years will prove to create problems in your new world. The first issue is quantity. Most of us learned a long time ago that it was more economical to purchase certain things in large supplies. Things such as paper towels in 12 packs and laundry detergent in the largest container available. Purchasing in this manor also decreased the number of trips we had to make to the market. RV'ers must find a quantity that they

can store in their RV and learn to live with it. They also
need to become comfortable with shopping more
frequently. RV'ers generally will shop at least once a week.
Our refrigerators are wonderful but they are not as efficient
as those big beautiful appliances we had in our homes.
This also means you can't expect produce to last as long as
it did before. Planning meals becomes more important
than it ever was. Fortunately, you will have more time to
do that planning as you don't have to worry about mowing
the lawn.

One suggestion we have is to shop in stores that are
familiar and you can depend on them for the items you use
frequently. Many RV'ers shop at Wal*Mart, Kmart and
other such chain markets. You generally can find the
things you depend on and most of the stores are laid out in
a similar fashion. It is much easier to be efficient and get
everything you need when you don't have to search for the
canned corn. We don't want to discourage you from
exploring any of the unusual shops however. We have
found many intriguing shops along the way. Recently we
stopped by a farmer's market style produce store and
found it to be full of wonderful homemade jams, jellies and
soups. The local Amish community sold the products of
their gardens as well as their kitchens in this quaint little
shop. The prices were great, the freshness was terrific and
the homemade items were a pure delight. Local farmers
markets and road side stands also provide a wonderful

option for local produce. The items you buy from these venders will last longer in your fridge than those purchased at a supermarket as they are generally much fresher.

Another option for shopping is the large chain warehouse style stores such as Costco and Sam's Club. Both of these examples charge an annual membership fee. It is important however to be cautious that you don't purchase more than you can store. Those packages of steaks at Costco will scream your name and are hard to resist. The quality is excellent however we have gotten home with one of those huge packages of meat and not had room for it in our small freezer. Once again we suggest pre-planning your purchases. One last trick is to repackage these purchases when you get home, into plastic bags. Many people have invested in the vacuum storage systems. They swear by them and they mold into the space much easier than the foam trays you purchase your meats in.

Hair care

Haircuts and other hair care will offer another challenge. Most people have always had someone in their community that they depended on to provide this service. When you travel for long periods of time, you don't have that luxury. Many couples have turned to cutting each other's hair. It is not uncommon to see a couple sitting outside their RV with a pair of electric clippers. For those who aren't brave enough for this practice there are lots of inexpensive chain salons where you can get a reasonable hair cut and / or perm for a discount price. Additionally if you choose to shop at the Super Wal*Marts very often they have a salon within their walls.

Pets

If you are considering traveling with your pets, and we strongly encourage that you do, you should know a couple of things. Most parks will not accept certain breeds of dogs, such as Rotweilers, Pit Bulls, Chows, German Sheppard's or Dobermans. Most parks will not allow more than 2 dogs of any size. Most parks will not allow "exotic pets" of any type. Some parks require that you present evidence that your pets have current vaccinations. We carry a copy of the rabies certificates in our reservation binder. If you are planning to travel into Mexico or Canada they require that proof as well. Remember that your pets need protection from heartworm, fleas and ticks even if you don't usually worry about them at home. It is very important to talk to your vet about this. We purchase a supply of medications from the veterinarian depending how long we will be away from our home base. One of our pets has had several bouts of illness and is on daily medications. We spent a good deal of time talking to our vet about our adventure and he gave us a letter that he prepared detailing the health history of our precious Jill. This way we have accurate information to present in the event that we need to find medical care for her while away from home.

Pet Grooming

Many people have learned how to groom their pets themselves. There are several video tapes as well as books that will assist you in this task. You can find everything you will need in the larger pet supply stores. We attempted this as well but found that our yorkies behaved very badly when we attempted to groom them. Additionally the bath and hair cut are not the only service the groomer performs. They clean the hair out of their ears, trim their nails and clean the anal gland. Not everyone is able to pull this off. If you find you are not going to take this step in self sufficiency, you will need to find groomers along the way. Many communities have the large chain pet supply stores such as PetsMart and Petco. They offer grooming services on site. We have had good luck with the quality of the grooming but found them to be a bit expensive. These franchise type groomers require you to present record of the pet's vaccinations. Another option is to inquire of other people in the park and / or the park staff. Frequently they have information on groomers who are close to the park and accept traveling pets. We have also consulted with the local humane society or SPCA for a recommendation. Generally they are happy to give you advice and certainly they have the best information available, as they often are the agency to investigate complaints.

GPS / Navigation

We highly suggest that you invest in a software program or buy a navigation system. There are many different programs available and we suggest you look into several before making a purchase. The product we chose is called Co-Pilot. It is a version especially designed for RV's. This means it will steer you around or away from low bridges, tight turns and the like. It even has an option of Canadian travel you can add on. This particular program is loaded on your laptop and sits on the dashboard. Your RV may already have a GPS system in it and we highly suggest you learn to use it. We also use maps, directions from books, directions we get from the park over the phone and map quest. We generally consider at least two sources just to assure ourselves that we are still on the right road. Of course, you have to keep your eye on the signs as you are driving so the audio version is actually helpful. We have followed written directions that tell you to make a left turn at the Piggy Wiggley grocery store only to find that it burned down a year ago. The Co-pilot system runs about $199 at Camping World and I think that may have saved our marriage as Nadine is a lousy navigator. She flunked map reading as well and didn't take the summer school make up class.

Mail service

As good as the internet is you will still have occasion to deal with "snail mail", you know, the paper stuff of days gone by. You need to make arrangements for your mail before you head out. You need to coordinate your mail, your driver's license, vehicle registration and medical insurance. There are many choices if you decide to use a mailbox or mail forwarding service. Some are rather expensive and others are more reasonable. One important consideration is the frequency that they forward your mail to you and just what will be forwarded. Most offer you a sorting service for an additional fee. This means they will sort through mail and discard the items that you don't want to receive (such as catalogues or advertisement flyers). If they don't sort this and they charge postage for the packages they send to you, you could be paying a hefty bill for things you don't want. The US Postal service offers a mail forwarding service, but has limitations on how often you can change your address. Remember not all parks accept mail, so there are times you will need to have mail held until you reach someplace where you can receive it. Another option is to arrange for a friend or relative to receive your mail. Personally we chose that option. On occasion we receive checks in the mail and our arrangements allow our daughter or son-in-law to deposit them into our bank.

Additionally, we plan a telephone conversation where we go through the mail with them. We can have them forward something right away, give us information from it or discard it. We supplied them with a stamp for endorsing checks and deposit slips. We purchased a supply of envelopes and stamps for sending things along to us. We even preprinted labels for sending checks to the bank. Additionally they picked up a supply of free US Mail Priority envelopes from the post office at no charge. These are 11" X 14" and she can stuff them full without regard to weight. The fee is under $4.00 no matter how much she puts inside. We contacted the magazines we had had subscriptions to and canceled them and notified the companies that sent catalogues to us that we wanted our names removed from their lists. We are sad to say that this effort fell on deaf ears. Our daughter loves to tell us about the amazing volume of catalogues that we still receive at her address. Many are from companies we have never heard of! We are very pleased with our system. Of course you will need to make a decision as to what is best for you and your circumstances.

5 – THINGS TO DO AND SEE

This great country of ours has an overwhelming selection of wonders just waiting for someone to explore and enjoy. Naturally we asked the good folks who responded to our survey where they most enjoyed traveling and received a broad overview of some of these US treasures. We find that most people spend about a week in any one area to explore. There are so many places to travel to that you just might not be able to get to all of them in a lifetime. Naturally there are some things that will spark your interest more than others. It is important that you talk about the things that you want to explore, as you might find that you may in fact share these interests with your spouse or significant other and didn't even know it. Recently we learned during a causal conversation with friends that both of us were fascinated by old cemeteries. We had missed several great opportunities to see some wonderful cemeteries because neither of us had mentioned it to the other. You can bet we have rectified that omission in our exploring.

Most people who responded to our survey speak of a strong desire to visit warm climates, beaches and as one person stated, "any place where there is no snow". Alaska is still a favorlte of many but most tell us they pick the month they travel to Alaska very carefully. For the most part people are fascinated with the rich history of our

great nation.   The eastern states offer as much of this‾
type of touring as you can work into your itinerary.   We
recently traveled through almost all of the Eastern states
and found that they provide more beautiful architecture
and historic areas than one could possible visit in one trip.
It's one thing to read about it but actually seeing places
like Gettysburg and Savannah are awe inspiring.

One suggestion we have when traveling to a new city or
area that you are unfamiliar with is to consider taking a
narrated tour first. Many cities offer tours conducted by a
company identifying them as "Trolley Tours" while others
use buses or train type vehicles. Our rational is that you
have a wonderful narrirated tour of the area allowing you
to get a lay of the land and some idea of places you want
to go back to later. You can then spend more of your time
seeing the sights and less driving around lost.   This is a
good time to mention that many full-timers haul their
bikes around and find they can cover a lot of ground in
less time while getting valuable exercise.   There are a
wide variety of bicycle types that you will see.   Naturally
the usual multi gear style bike still predominates but they
are being challenged by the return of the old fashioned
one gear, handles up, larger seat style bikes that are very
available in most stores at modest prices.   Some people
have chosen the three-wheel version of the bicycle,
allowing them to be more stable when traveling on rough
roads and paths. We were intrigued by the many folks who

attach their golf clubs (on a pull cart) to their bikes for towing to the links. One woman we saw actually towed a wheeled cart with her laundry to and from the laundry. Storing your bike can generally be accomplished by the use of a bike rack either on your tow car or the ladder in the back of your RV. Some folks have a hitch installed that allows them to use that type of bike rack. Many people are moving to the battery-operated scooters to get around. They are naturally heavier and more difficult to transport.

The following is a selection of the actual answers we received with our survey about places to go:

Favorite Places to Travel: Warm, Sunny, Bug Free, West, Southwest, Mississippi, West, Northwest, Wyoming, South Dakota, South in Winter, Northeast in summer/fall, National Parks, Beaches, Forests, Nevada, N. Calif., Arizona, Alaska and, any place where there is no snow. Others said, Rocky Mountains, Mexico, Oregon Coast and Canada. As you can see just about anyplace we can drive to is worth a visit depending upon the time of year.

One of the common joys we all share is good food. In our survey we asked the responders to tell us of favorite, even unusual places they had eaten. We received some intriguing responses. We have even managed to find some of them ourselves and agree that they were worth the search. Different people have different tastes in food as with everything else in life. One thing for sure, you will find most of the really memorable restaurants in the least likely places. Many people find the most interesting and pleasurable food by asking the locals.   However we don't want to discourage your exploring some of the famous places as well. They got that fame by being very special. One good example is Lamberts "The home of throwed rolls". They are advertised heavily and are found in 4 or 5 locations in the south and southwest. They offer an unusual experience and amazing food. A word of caution is to be careful how you ask for more rolls. You just might find yourself ducking a buttery yeasty bun as it zings by your ear.

Some of the responses we received from our survey are listed here:

Unusual and favorite Places You've Eaten: Space Alien Hamburger in ND, What Locals Recommend, Moe's on the Oregon coast, Hammerhead Grill in Rhode Island, The GA Pig in Brunswick, GA, Tundra Inn in Churchill, MN, Otis Café in Otis, Oregon, Strouds in KC, Arthur Bryants BQ in KC, Yellowknife in Circle, Utah where they supply a fly swatter with the menu, Lamberts in Foley AL (Home of Throwed Rolls), Sushi in Wisconsin, Great Mexican in Texas, Cracker Barrel, Black Beard's on Jekyll Island, GA, The Snake Pit in Idaho, Beyond Hope in Idaho, One Eyed Lizzy's in Savannah, Sea Hag in Depot Bay Oregon, No Name Pub in Big Pine Key, Florida, Sloppy Joes in Key West to name a few.

What to do while traveling? This is a very broad question. Naturally touring, and sight seeing top the charts. Many people customize their travels with the pursuit of the things that interest them. We will list some of the responses we received. It is important to consider what you will do in the time that you are not traveling or touring a museum. Many people have hobbies that they enjoy and find they can still pursue despite limited storage space. We are always amazed at the hobbies and activities that people find a way to incorporate into their new lifestyle. Reading and game playing are wonderful ways to enjoy some of that time you will find you have more of. Don't forget that when you are staying in the large RV Parks they may have more planned activities than you could possibly work into your day. We often tell folks that if they aren't doing something, it is their own fault. Did we mention the activity of simply meeting new people and enjoying the socializing? Many of the parks actually have social events to encourage the guests to meet each other.

Some of the survey responses we received:

Favorite Activities While Traveling: Hiking, Biking, Relaxing, Internet, town-to-town, Touring Factories, Theme Parks, Auto Museums, National Parks, Golf, Sightseeing, Petroglypsh, Pictography, Riding Motorcycles, Visiting Air Bases, Fishing, Volunteering, Cross Stitching, Puzzles, Reading, Finding Auto Race Tracks, painting and crafting, finding the diamonds in our back yard. RVing is a great alternative to Mexico, Hawaii, etc., Travel, Doing volunteer work, Work with religious groups and Spending time with people with like interests.

There is a lot to do and see in this great country of ours and no better way to see it than traveling in an RV.

6 – SOME TERMINOLOGY

As you begin your research into living the full-timer lifestyle you will hear some terminology that may be confusing to you. We have listed some of the terminology just to give you a sense of what RVer's and RV sales people are talking about. RV Terminology is not extensive nor is it difficult to learn. So don't let the thought of having to learn a new language scare you away. We will include some web sites in the next chapter that will provide a more wide-ranging list of terminology.

Here are some examples:

Basement - refers to a storage area accessible from the outside of the motor home or trailer.

Black Tank - This is the holding tank for storing solid waste.

Boondocking – Also known as "dry camping" or "primitive camping", means to camp out without using the modern conveniences of hooking up to electric, sewer and water.

Braking System – refers to a brake system for a "Towed" vehicle. This is required in most states and we cannot stress enough the need to have a braking system for your own safety, the safety of others and the prevention of damage to your rig and towed vehicle.

Class A – Class of motor home referring to motor home (box) built on chassis frame up.

Class C – Class of motor home referring to an RV built using van-type chassis and cab.

Diesel Pusher – Term for rear engine diesel motor home.

Dinghy – Term for towed vehicle, also known as a "toad".

Fiver – Another name for fifth wheel trailer.

Full hookup – This is a term used by campgrounds providing full accommodations such as water, sewer/septic and electricity.

Fulltimer/Full-timer – People who travel and live in their recreational vehicle for most or all of the year.

Grey Tank – The holding tank for storing used dishwater and bath water.

Motorcoach – term for a motor home on a "bus-type" Chassis

Shore Power – Electricity provided by plugging in to an external power source such as the electrical hook-up from the campground power to your RV.

Slide-out – Additional living space that "slides out" either by hydraulics, electricity or manually, when RV is set up.

Snowbird – This is a term often used for someone living in a northern climate that heads "south" in the winter months.

Toad – Another term for a "towed" vehicle.

Wally World – Slang used by RVer's to describe Wal*Mart.

7 – SOME RESOURCES

As we have mentioned throughout the book there are a lot of resources and viewpoints on full-time RVing and how you should prepare. We hope that we have given you a reasonable insight into this emerging lifestyle and some useful tips to help you along your way. Here are some web sites that we feel might be helpful as you prepare for an exciting new adventure:

For terminology try:

rvadvice.com

mytravco.com

Most of the information is the same but they each have a few different terminologies.

For general information try:

campingworld.com – go to resources to access forum

rv.net

ftrv.com

woodalls.com

movinon.net

trailerlife.com

Search Full-Time RVing via google or another search engine.

Talk to as many people as possible.

Budget work sheet

Items	Monthly expense	Comments
Rent (fee for parking)		
Payments on RV and/or tow vehicle		
Health Insurance		
Auto / RV insurance		
Mail forwarding service		
Medications		
Cell phone service		
Fuel		
Food		
Vehicle up keep		
Entertainment		
Internet service		
Satellite TV service		
On line banking fees		
License and registration of vehicles		
Drivers licenses		
Membership fees for discount plans		

Really simple, just add in the amounts you will need to spend, and subtract from money you will have available each month. Naturally you will add or subtract to meet your personal situation.

Making Reservations

Information you need to have available	Example
Dates	Arrive Aug. 1, depart Aug. 7
Number of nights staying	6 nights
Discount plan you want to use	Passport America, page 154
Fee you anticipate	$11.00 per night
Type of vehicle	Motor Home
Length of vehicle	40 feet
Number of sliders	3
Number of adults in party	2

Information you will need to have available before calling or emailing for reservations.

Date

You need to know when you will arrive and when you will depart. Parks charge for nights you stay so using the term depart will assure that you are on the same page as the park.

Number of nights

Count only the nights you will stay in the park.

Discount

The plan you are using. We keep track of the plan and the page it is found on in the book. This makes referring to it quick and easy especially as you are traveling down the road.

Fee

Note the fee you anticipate paying per night. Remember any book or site you use may not have the most updated rates but it gives you a starting point.

Type of vehicle

The park will want to know the type of RV, length, number of sliders and often the age of your RV as some parks have a maximum age that they will accept (such as 10 years or less).

Number in party

The park will want to know how many adults and children in your party as some charge a surcharge for extra people. They want to know about your pets as well. Please refer to the chapter on pets as there are a few rules you must consider.

Worksheet to use when making Reservations

Question	Answer
Can you make reservations for dates you desire?	
What is the daily rate (or weekly or monthly or season)	
Are there extra charges?	
Does quote include taxes?	
What is check in time?	
Name of person taking your call.	
Confirmation number	
Will you have full hookups?	
What amp service do they have?	
Do they accept credit cards?	
Deposit	
Remaining fee due	
Discount plan you want to use.	

Fees

If you plan to stay longer than a few days, you will want to ask about a discounted rate for weekly, monthly and season. You should ask if the rate includes tax or is that additional.

Extra Charges

Remember they may have charges you don't see in the book.

Check in time

Occasionally we have found parks that state that there is a fee for arriving and taking your site before the official check in time. It is important to give them your estimated arrival time to assure that someone will be available to check you in. We have found that some parks close rather early and do not accept guests who arrive after 3 or 4 in the afternoon.

Method of payment

Confirm with the person you are making reservations with that they will accept your choice of payment options. Some parks will require cash only for one or two night stays. They want to avoid charges by the credit card company and are not accepting personal checks to avoid having them returned.

Payment

Make note of amount of deposit and amount remaining that you owe the park. This information should be kept handy so that you are sure the amount they request at check in is the amount you agreed to.

8 – SOME FINAL THOUGHTS

When RV'ers get together they often discuss their travels and lifestyle choice. We have enjoyed lively conversations with people who have been full-timing for many years and those who were still in the decision making phase. There is always something to learn and something to share. We have found that almost everyone we have met is delighted to share his or her opinions regarding almost anything. We love that most RV'ers are so open and helpful. They gladly lend a hand or advice. Most RV'ers are very dependable and honest. It is extremely rare to hear that someone had a bad experience with other RV'ers. Naturally, you take precautions, just like you did in your previous life; you lock your doors and secure your treasurers. You are aware of your surroundings and if you feel uncomfortable about a place or situation you just use those wheels and move!

Recently we spent a wonderful evening with a couple who are still working on their decision to sell their home and travel full-time or to keep the house and travel intermittently. They like many others decided to spend a lengthy period traveling in their RV to get some idea of what full-timing feels like. It is a highly recommended plan especially when there is a difference in opinion between the two parties.

There are many issues that each full-timer must address if they are going to make the transition from the traditional type of life to full-timing. Additionally, there are many variations that you can choose. Some people keep a home and travel off and on. Others maintain a home in the northern areas where winter can be harsh. They "winter" in the warm states like Florida, Texas, Arizona and California. Some even go to Mexico for the winter months. How you design your new life is dependant on finances and personal choice.

Take your time to make a decision. Many people make a commitment to delay making a permanent decision for several years. This delay allows you to consider a wide variety of choices and factor experiences into the decision. Some people never make a hard and fast decision on how their new life will be structured. If this sounds too much like floating through life without goals, it is anything but. Your goal is to experience a new way of living and learning from the people you meet and the experiences you have. You will be able to customize your plan as you go. If you lock yourself into a tight plan too early, you just might find yourself in a place you don't want to be.

One element that everyone must reconcile with themselves is learning that full-timing is a delicious combination of travel, resting, learning, exploring and socializing. The one thing it is not is a *vacation*. By the time we begin considering the full-timing option, we have become well trained in the working lifestyle. You learn that relaxing and travel are generally reserved for vacations and long weekends. You know that you have a block of time to accomplish your vacation goals and then it is "back to reality". Not to mention that you plan your finances accordingly for a vacation. Your new reality in the full-timing world is that you have dramatically reduced daily responsibilities and greatly increased amounts of time to do that which makes you happy. If you don't get it done today, you can do it tomorrow. Not that you become the type of person who never accomplishes anything. Indeed, you simply find that you have the time to do those things you have longed to do for so many years. You become comfortable with leaving the dishes to spend the day on a beautiful beach and save the dishes for bad weather. The options are infinite. They range from doing nothing but watching the grass grow to volunteering with a group to build Habitat for Humanity houses. We have found that we are never bored and always busy. You most likely will find that your path will be somewhere down the middle and is customized just for you.

To summarize, if you are considering the full-timing approach to retirement you have a great many decisions to make. You must give a good deal of time and thought to formulating a plan. You must above all be sure that if you are a couple that you both are on the same page. To enter this process without good strong communication will place you at risk of making a serious error. We highly recommend that anyone considering this life style do as much research as possible. Talk to people, read books and test out your plans. Make alternate plans based on variations that you might anticipate. Talking and planning, they are the two most important things you can do to insure that you design your retirement to be perfect and customized just for you.

Not unlike the previous version of your life, you will make mistakes. But just like most other things, you just change directions and find the right path.

RV'ing is an amazing equalizer. Most of the people you meet will carry on a lengthy conversation without ever asking about the type of work you did before you made the big change. Status is not important and while it certainly is not off limits, it is often not discussed in casual conversation. As you read in the results of the survey, the vocations of the responders vary greatly. Full-timing offers a wonderful common ground for most people.

Now, the rest is up to you. Whatever route you choose to go take time to enjoy life and savor the fruits of our great country. You won't be disappointed.

07/01/—

Printed in the United States
66149LVS00007B/236

9 781847 289803